eXplore

BUDDY,
RAT TERMINATOR
A Little Friend with a Big Heart
Sharlene G. Coombs

KNOWLEDGE
BOOKS

Teacher Notes:

Terriers like Buddy make great pets, but did you know that they are also great rat terminators? Join the author as she talks about the role of different working dogs and how these fearless little terriers have kept communities safe from rodents for many years.

Discussion points for consideration:

1. Discuss all the different kinds of working dogs you can think of and what they do.

2. Discuss the meaning of humane – why is poison a crueler death for rodents?

3. More and more careers today involve working with dogs – discuss this further.

Difficult words to be introduced and practiced before reading this book:

Tenterfield, Terrier, Jack Russell, differences, shivering, service, soldiers, dangerous, Ukraine, Russian, invasion, fearless, vermin, instinct, plague, machinery, expensive, Government, volunteer, humane, England, hygiene, conditions, disease, bacteria, infected, quarantine, rhyme, technology, Brisbane, Queensland, threatened.

Contents

1. Meet Buddy!

This cute little dog is my best friend. His name is Buddy. He is a Tenterfield Terrier.

There are many different breeds of terriers. You may know Jack Russell or Fox Terriers. Buddy is a bit like those dogs. The main differences are his longer legs and longer snout.

Buddy is 12 years old. This is quite old for a dog. However, his age hasn't slowed him down at all!

Buddy has always been very active. He loves chasing the ball. Sometimes I have to hide the ball to make him have a rest.

He also chases the hose and loves to swim. He jumps in my sister's pool, even in winter! He comes out shivering but still goes back in.

Buddy has also learned a new trick. He dives for rocks in the water! He can dive a long way under the water to find a rock. He's such a clever little dog!

5

2. Why Tenterfield?

Tenterfield is a small town in NSW, Australia. It is famous because of the song "The Tenterfield Saddler".

A man called George Woolnough worked there as a saddler for many years. The song was written for George by his famous grandson, Peter Allen.

George made saddles for riding horses. He also had terriers as pets. They would go everywhere with him. This is how the Tenterfield Terrier got its name!

A FEDERATION TOWN
ESTABLISHED 1851

Tenterfield

THE BIRTHPLACE OF OUR NATION

PARTNER
OTTOBE
HAWANGEN
GERM

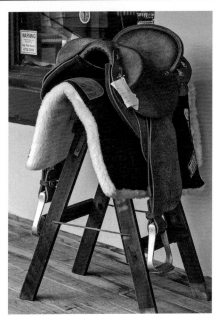

3. Working Dogs

Buddy is a very smart dog. In fact, most terriers are very smart. This is why they make great working dogs.

There are many different types of working dogs today. Dogs can be very helpful to many people. Some dogs are service dogs. Labradors make good guide dogs for blind people.

Police dogs are called K-9s. They have been trained to help the police in their jobs. Can you think of any other working dogs?

Some working dogs have been trained to work in war zones. They work with the soldiers and have dangerous jobs.

Have you heard about a brave little Jack Russell Terrier called Patron? He has been helping the people of Ukraine. Patron has been trained to find landmines left from the Russian invasion.

A soldier takes him into the war zones to sniff out the bombs. The bombs are cleared, and the area is safe again. Since the start of the Ukraine war, little Patron has sniffed out over 230 bombs. He was even given a medal for his brave service!

4. Great Hunters!

Terriers are a very old dog breed. People have been using them as working dogs for hundreds of years.

Some terriers make good guard dogs. They let their owners know if someone is there. They may be small, but they are fearless.

Their most common job has been to hunt vermin. This includes rats, mice, rabbits, and foxes. Why do you think they are such good vermin hunters?

The word terrier comes from an old word that means earth or ground. Terriers would often go underground to chase animals. This is how the terrier breed got its name.

Their small size was important. It helped them to chase rabbits out of burrows. It also helped them to get into tight spots where rats and mice were hiding.

Many terriers still work on farms today. They help their owners keep the rodents away.

Rodents move very fast. One of the reasons why terriers are such great hunters is their speed. They are super quick!

Terriers also have something called a prey drive. This is their need to chase, catch, and kill small animals like rats and mice.

This prey drive is not taught to them. They are born with it. It is also called instinct.

Terriers are small dogs, but they are very strong. They also have very strong jaws. This helps them to kill their prey quickly. This way, the animal doesn't suffer.

When Buddy kills a rat, he grabs it behind the neck. He bites quickly and shakes it at the same time. This breaks the rat's neck. It doesn't feel anything after that.

5. Rat Invasion!

In 2021, many farms in Australia had rat and mice plagues. After a great harvest, there was plenty of food for the rats and mice. The good weather also helped.

The mice moved across the country quickly. They ate crops and grain. They damaged hay bales that were meant to feed cattle. They even started eating the wires in farm machinery!

As winter came and the nights got colder, they started looking for warm places to hide. They found their way into cars and ate the seats and wires. They even ate plastic! They also made nests and had many babies.

People couldn't keep the rats and mice out of their houses. They found their way inside through tiny holes. They ate everything, including books. Nests were made in all sorts of places.

Farmers had to put out rodent bait every day. This took hours, but it still wasn't helping. It was also very expensive. Before too long, the shops ran out of the bait.

The plagues grew bigger because the rodents bred so quickly. Finally, the Government helped the farmers by giving them free poison. This helped to kill the rodents quickly. It took a long time before it was all under control.

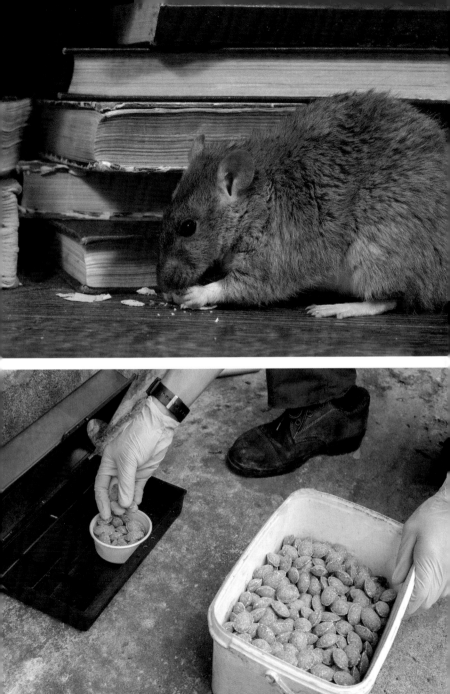

6. Call In the Rat Pack!

In 2020 in England, a pig farmer had a big rat problem. He had tried everything, and nothing was working. The rats just kept breeding and eating the pig feed.

He called in the Suffolk and Norfolk Rat Pack. The Rat Pack is a volunteer group of people. They own different terrier dogs. They take their dogs onto farms to help get rid of rats. It's also much more humane than using poison.

When the Rat Pack got the call from the farmer, they soon found out how big the problem was. Within seconds of arriving at the farm, the dogs could smell the rats. They went crazy!

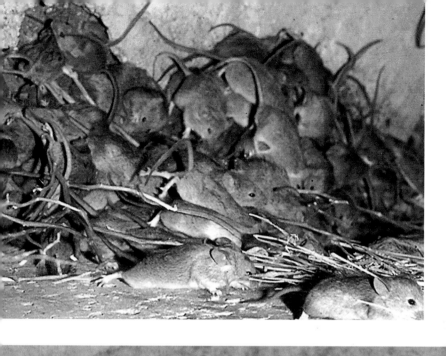

25

Their prey drive kicked in. They worked together as a team to sniff them out. Their owners helped dig holes to find the rats. It was a team effort.

The rats were very fast and some of them were almost as big as the dogs! However, the terriers were faster. As each rat appeared, it was killed within seconds.

The fearless little terriers worked for over 7 hours that day and killed 730 rats! This was one of their biggest hauls ever. The terriers loved it and the farmer was very happy.

7. The Great Plague of London

Hundreds of years ago in England, The Great Plague killed 100,000 people in London alone. It killed millions more across the world.

Back then, hygiene was poor, and the city was filthy. People didn't have toilets like we do now. They threw their waste into the streets.

Rats loved these dirty conditions. They bred quickly. Soon there were millions of rats living in cities like London.

THE 'BLACK DEATH'
ENTERED ENGLAND IN 1348
THROUGH THIS PORT.

IT KILLED 30-50%
OF THE COUNTRY'S
TOTAL POPULATION

How did the plague begin? Some people thought that the rats carried the disease. This wasn't true. The rats carried fleas. The fleas that lived on the rats carried deadly bacteria.

When people were bitten by the fleas, they got very sick with the plague disease. As the rats moved from town to town, they carried the infected fleas with them. This is how the plague spread so far and wide.

The infected people also spread the disease to other people close by, through coughing and sneezing. Most infected people died.

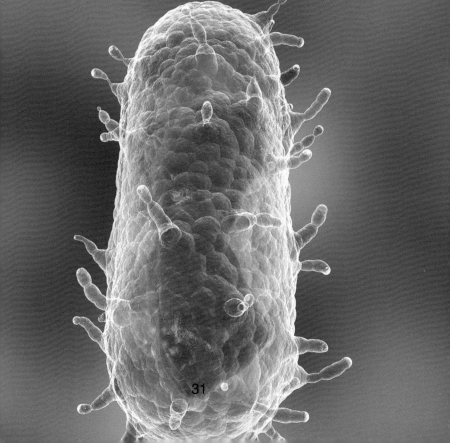

31

In those days, people didn't know that the fleas were causing the disease. Some people thought that God had sent the disease to punish them. They also didn't realise that it was being spread from person to person.

Once they learned more about it, the Government made some rules to help stop the spread. Plague doctors went door to door checking for people with the disease. Infected people had to stay in their homes. This stopped them spreading it to others in the city.

This is called quarantine. It helps to stop the disease from spreading. However, they couldn't stop the rats that carried the infected fleas. The plague only really stopped when a great fire burned most of London to the ground.

Have you heard the nursery rhyme, "Ring Around the Rosy"? This rhyme is about the Great Plague. The words from the rhyme talk about the signs of the disease in people.

The first signs of the plague in people were red spots on their skin – the "ring". "A pocket full of posies" are the small flowers people carried. They thought they would stop the infection.

"Atishoo, atishoo" are the sneezes that many people had. "We all fall down" is when the person died from the plague. It's not such a happy nursery rhyme after all!

8. Modern Day Rat Problems

Cities have changed a lot over the years. They are now planned better. New technology has made it safer and cleaner to live in big cities.

However, cities still have rodent problems. With big cities comes lots of rubbish. Rodents love rubbish.

Big cities also have plenty of places for rodents to hide. New York City has 2 million rats, and for every 2 million people living in Paris, there are 4 million rats!

Brisbane is the capital city of Queensland in Australia. It's a big city with over 2.5 million people. Did you know that terriers have been used to hunt and kill rodents in Brisbane for over 100 years?

From 1900 to 1909, the Black Plague threatened Brisbane. The Government had to do something quickly. They knew that rats carried the fleas which carried the plague.

They started the terrier rat gang to help kill the rats. It was a risky job, but it started working. These brave little terriers helped to stop the Black Plague.

These days, Brisbane City Council has a special rodent control team. The terriers have been trained to sniff out rodent nests.

The team visits over 1,500 homes and businesses each year. Once they find the nest, the owners can get rid of the rodents.

Dogs make life easier for humans in so many ways. They make amazing pets, and they also make great working dogs. No wonder we call them "man's best friend"!

Word Bank

Tenterfield
Terrier
Jack Russell
differences
shivering
service
soldiers
dangerous
Ukraine
Russian
invasion
fearless
vermin
instinct
plague
machinery
expensive

Government
volunteer
humane
England
hygiene
conditions
disease
bacteria
infected
quarantine
rhyme
technology
Brisbane
Queensland
threatened